Laura Secord

John M. Bassett
A. Roy Petrie

A Canadian Heroine

Fitzhenry & Whiteside Limited

Contents

© 1974 Fitzhenry & Whiteside Limited
150 Lesmill Road,
Don Mills, Ontario, M3B 2T5

Printed in Canada

ISBN 0-88902-202-X

Laura Secord Chapter 1
Looks Back

The little old lady sat quietly beside the fire in the ladder-back chair. Her plain black dress was buttoned up tightly at the neck. Its dark colour was relieved by the white bonnet tied by a large bow under her chin. The lace mittens she wore were also white.

Laura Secord in old age

The lady was ninety-three years old. One might well wonder how so frail a person could have survived the harsh life of the frontier to reach this great age. But a closer look at the old lady suggested that she was not as frail as at first appeared. She held herself erect, and her eyes were alert. The smile on her lips showed courage and determination, as well as humour.

It was 1868, one year after the birth of Canada as a nation. In the preceding ninety years, this lady had seen her country develop from a wilderness to a prosperous land. But she had seen far more than that. She had seen war, invasion and rebellion, and been ready to help her country whenever and wherever possible. Indeed, it is probable that Canada owed her a debt that could never be paid.

What was she thinking about? Her memory might have gone to her youth, recalling the dangers and hardships of coming to a harsh frontier. Perhaps she thought of her husband and of the children she had outlived. But no bitterness spoilt the memories of those distant days when she faced great danger to carry the message that was so important to her country's safety.

This lady was Laura Secord. On one of the tablets that records her brave act are these words: A HEROINE OF UPPER CANADA WHO SAVED HER COUNTRY FROM THE ENEMY IN 1813.

Chapter 2 The Secords

In 1776, revolution broke out in Britain's American Colonies. For several reasons, many colonists were determined to break all connections with the British by force.

War at any time is cruel, and a revolution is especially horrible. People are forced to take sides, and sometimes father fights son, and brother fights brother.

The American Revolution proved no exception. The choice was not an easy one. On the one hand, a person could remain loyal to a king three thousand miles away, who often showed little regard for his American subjects; or one could support the Patriots, who sometimes confused independence with a chance to loot a neighbour's house.

By 1783, the Loyalists (those who remained loyal to the British Crown) were finally defeated. But before the end of the war, in order to save their lives, they were forced to leave home, wealth, and property, and run. The Niagara frontier, almost a total wilderness, was one of the few places the Loyalists could run to.

In November, 1776, the first of thousands of Loyalists came to Niagara. The large canoe, paddled by a few friendly Indians, carried five women and thirty-one children. One of the children, three-year-old James Secord, was later to marry Laura Ingersoll.

James was the youngest of his family. His father, Lieutenant James Secord, and two of his brothers were fighting in Colonel John Butler's Rangers. Butler's Rangers were a group of Loyalist soldiers who roamed New York State, to save as many Loyalists as they could and bring them to the safety of Niagara.

The Secord family was given a tent, clothing and food. More than one woman wept, "What have we come to?" But the courage that had helped them escape helped them settle in this new country.

Many women had brought cuttings from apple, peach, and plum trees, and a variety of berry bushes. In a few years, the trees and bushes grew to maturity. Today, in the fruit orchards of the Niagara Peninsula, can be seen the results of their foresight.

John Butler

James' father fought in eight battles as a Loyalist. As a reward, he was given six hundred acres of land. Showing all the skill of a farmer, miller, and mechanic, he set about making a home for his family in Niagara.

The old Secord cabin

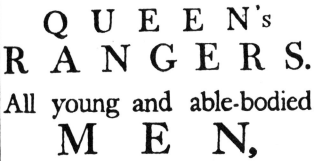

*"The Falls of Niagara" drawn
by Father Hennepin, the first
European to see them*

The arrival of the Loyalists
In what ways were the
newcomers unsuited for life on
the frontier?

The Ingersolls Chapter 3

The Ingersolls came to Canada in quite different circumstances from the Secords. Laura Ingersoll was born on September 13, 1775, in Great Barrington, a town in Massachusetts, in the United States. During the American Revolution, the Ingersolls threw in their lot with the Patriots. Unlike the Secords, who had to flee for their lives, the Ingersolls at first reaped the rewards of being on the winning side.

Thomas Ingersoll, Laura's father, was made a major in the United States Army. His business prospered, and he hoped to enlarge it by borrowing large sums of money. It is not surprising that Laura's father did well. Ingersolls had been in that part of New England for almost two hundred years. They were well-known as exceptionally clever men. The family included inventors, mechanics, merchants, magistrates, teachers, and soldiers.

Unfortunately for Thomas Ingersoll, a severe depression swept the United States shortly after the end of the war. Ingersoll had over-borrowed; work as he might, he saw that it would be impossible to regain his former state of prosperity. Restless and energetic, he sought a way out of his difficulties.

He remembered a conversation that he had had some years before with the great Indian Chief, Joseph Brant. Something about Ingersoll had attracted the Indian, who had pressed him to come to Canada. "Come, my son, where the land is rich, the rivers filled with fish, and the forests with game. Leave this city and come to my land, where the air is fresh and life is good. I shall find you the best land in Canada."

Joseph Brant

Ingersoll had never made the slightest pretence of being loyal to the Crown. Some people blamed Governor Simcoe for offering land to people like him, who, only a few years before, had fought the British. But Simcoe knew that Canada must be settled and he rightly guessed that a man's love of the land he owned would guide his loyalties.

When, years later, war with the United States broke

out again, people such as Thomas Ingersoll, who had come to Canada for the land grants, were almost all loyal to the British Crown. Simcoe had judged correctly in inviting Americans to come to help open up Canada.

The land was sold to Thomas Ingersoll and his friends for only sixpence an acre. Sixty-six thousand acres of the fertile land near the River Thames were set aside for this group.

Unfortunately, once again Thomas Ingersoll failed financially. He was obliged to give up the land that had promised so much. Years later, his sons reclaimed it. The sons prospered and, in memory of their father, named the principal town after him: the present-day city of Ingersoll.

Loyalists drawing lots for their lands

*An early map of a settlement
showing the various lots and
their owners' names*

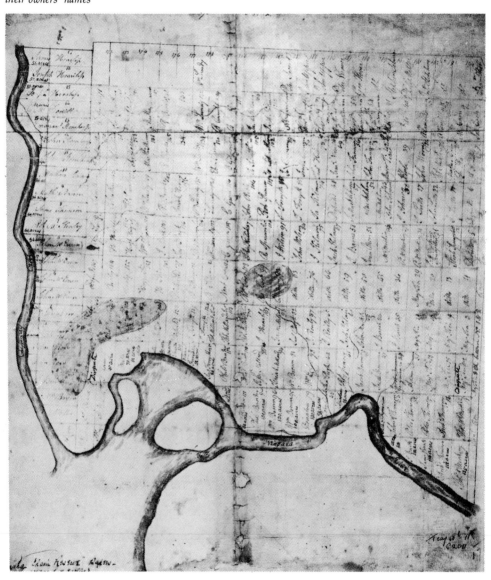

Early Days in Canada

Chapter 4

The Ingersolls came to Canada when Laura, the eldest child, was eighteen.

Her mother had died when she was eight. Her father married again, and she was responsible for the welfare of her many brothers and sisters. The journey was long, dangerous, and uncomfortable. The family travelled by canal, cart, and schooner from Massachusetts to the Niagara frontier. The last section, by schooner along Lake Ontario, should have been the most pleasant. However, a violent storm blew up, and the schooner was almost wrecked. Luckily, the travellers, although wet and hungry, managed to reach land safely.

Laura put her arm around her sobbing sister. "We'll soon be there, Elizabeth, and we'll get into dry clothes and get some hot food. Remember what father said about it: a paradise, a real paradise."

Laura was called upon throughout her entire life to encourage and help her family and friends. How someone who appeared to be so fragile could continually be a source of strength to others remained a mystery to the end of her days. But Laura's character was stronger than her body.

Thomas Ingersoll had been right about the land. It was indeed a paradise. The slips from peach, cherry, and plum trees, planted by the first settlers, had taken root, and the first harvest soon followed. The streams supplied a variety of fish, the most popular being freshwater salmon. The woods were filled with game, and the skillful hunter always returned with enough meat for his family.

Clearing land

"I like it here," said Thomas Ingersoll. "My land's up on the Thames and it is good, but we'll open a shop here at Queenston until we have the land cleared up country." Queenston, the entrance to the Niagara Peninsula, was a thriving, growing town.

The quickest way to start a business was to open a tavern. With his five eldest children, Ingersoll had a readily available source of help. Once again, we can see Laura taking more than her share of the burden, since her father was busy developing his land grant.

A frequent visitor at Ingersoll's Tavern was James Secord. Young Secord had opened a shop dealing in women's wear and household appliances. But when business was slack, James Secord spent more and more time in the tavern.

"It's not the drink I go for," he said. "It's a pleasant place to be."

"Pleasant place, my foot," replied a friend. "'Tis Laura Ingersoll that's caught your eye. You'd better marry the lass so you can get back to your store before you go bankrupt."

James took the advice, and married Laura Ingersoll. The wedding probably took place in 1798. In the war that was coming, a great number of records were destroyed, so we know neither the exact place nor the date of the marriage.

But we do know that the couple prospered. Certainly Laura was a great help to James in his business. By 1812, the Secords had five children, two servants, a small but pleasant frame house and a prosperous store. Visitors to Queenston today can visit the Secord home. They will find it almost exactly as it was when Laura lived there.

Life was good, and it seemed that the future held nothing but happiness for James and Laura Secord and their family. But the clouds of war were forming, and, as we know, war brings suffering.

While life was hard for the newcomers, there were plenty of examples of those who had come to the Niagara frontier earlier and created a very successful way of life.

Robert Hamilton

The most outstanding of these early arrivals who had achieved much was the Honourable Robert Hamilton. He and his family had moved to the Niagara Peninsula before the American Revolution. The country then was a complete wilderness. However, Hamilton saw the potential wealth of the area and set up a trading post. By the time the Loyalists started arriving he was well established. He had a magnificent house built on the edge of the Niagara River, just downstream from the falls. The Hamiltons were both a source of envy to the newcomers and also an example of what could be accomplished in a few years.

Hamilton was involved in a number of activities but saw that the real wealth lay in land. Every Loyalist, man, woman, or child, who came to the Niagara frontier was given a two-hundred-acre tract of land. Unfortunately not everyone had the will or the skill to carve a farm out of the wilderness. Many abandoned farming to seek other pursuits. They sold the two hundred acres for anything between six pounds and a gallon of whisky. Robert Hamilton was always ready to buy this land, and at his death he had acquired over one hundred thousand acres.

Robert Hamilton contributed much to the new land. At one time or another he had a brewery, a distillery, a warehouse, a tannery, a trading post, and an inn. He still found time to serve on the first executive council in Upper Canada and retain that position for the rest of his life. He was the first judge in the area and a member of the Land Board.

His home, for some time the most handsome in the frontier, meant that he had to play host to every visitor who came to Niagara Falls. Among his guests were the Duke of Kent, later to be Queen Victoria's father, the Duc de la Rochefoucauld, who found Hamilton of excellent character; and Mrs. Simcoe, wife of the first Governor of Upper Canada, who was most impressed by the balcony that ran along the entire length of the house.

So well did Robert Hamilton and his family thrive, that his grandson was able to leave an estate valued at two million on his death.

James and Laura Secord must have dreamed of achieving even a small part of such success. While both did more than the average person is called upon to do, this kind of material success was to be denied them.

These pictures show the development of the earliest primitive shanty into a flourishing pioneer settlement

Africans Chapter 5
in Niagara

The Loyalists and those in search of cheap land were not the only people who flocked to the Niagara Peninsula at this time. There was a steady stream of Negroes who made their way to Canada to escape from the slavery that was their lot in the United States.

In 1793, Governor John Graves Simcoe, at a meeting of the Legislature, passed a bill outlawing slavery in the province of Upper Canada. This made Canada and Denmark, which had passed an anti-slavery bill the year before, the first two countries to outlaw the cruel practice.

Even so, the papers still ran advertisements like these:

Governor John Graves Simcoe

"Wanted to purchase, a negroe girl from 7 to 12 of good disposition."
"For-sale, a negroe man slave, 18 years old."
"All persons are forbidden to harbour my Indian slave Sal, as I am determined to prosecute any offenders to the utmost extent of the law and persons who suffer her to remain on their premises for half an hour will be taken as offending and dealt with accordingly."

However, slavery was gradually done away with, and Canada became a haven for those who sought to escape.

We know that, after their marriage, James and Laura Secord had two coloured servants. For a successful merchant this was customary. That the Secords loathed slavery must be evident from their characters.

As the number of slaves seeking sanctuary in Canada increased, trouble was bound to break out. This trouble revolved around a slave named Moseby who had escaped from Kentucky.

In his flight he had made off with one of his owner's horses. His master traced him to Niagara and demanded that he be returned to the United States as a horse thief. Moseby was put in the Niagara Jail to await the Governor's decision. In the meantime, blacks from all over flocked to Niagara and surrounded the jail. The townsfolk showed their sympathy by providing them with food and shelter.

Finally, Governor Bond Head made his decision: Moseby was to be turned over to the American authorities as a horse thief. All available constables were pressed into duty. The appearance of Moseby in a wagon outside the jail touched off a violent struggle between the blacks and the constables. Moseby managed to escape and was never heard of again. Unfortunately, two Negroes were killed by gunfire. Many others were arrested and lodged in jail till the outbreak of Mackenzie's Rebellion the next year. A coloured company was then formed and black prisoners were allowed to enlist. The company did excellent service during the brief uprising.

A picture from a Wanted poster for runaway slaves

War and the Chapter 6
Battle of
Queenston
Heights

During the spring of 1812, rumours of war grew steadily louder in the fast-growing, prosperous town of Queenston.

"I don't like it," said James to Laura one night, after the children had gone to bed. "I don't like it at all. There's a wild crowd in the States. They're all cock-a-hoop since they beat the British in their revolution."

Laura tried to calm him. "No one wants war. Why should they want to harm us? We have never hurt them."

"No, not us, but the British Navy has been pretty high-handed at sea. And if the Yanks want to hit at the British, we're the closest to them."

"I've heard you say often enough that, with General Brock in command, we have nothing to fear. What's happened to the General that you talk like that?"

"You're right, Laura. With Brock and his 49th Regiment, it will be a rough day for anyone who wants to cross the river. But I wish we had something more than that regiment of Irish soldiers."

"Stop worrying," said Laura. "No one is going to bother us here. You'll see."

But Laura was wrong. On June 1, 1812, the President of the United States declared war against Great Britain, and American troops marched on Canada.

Which president of the U.S. declared war in 1812. Why?

At first, under General Brock's inspired leadership, the British were successful. They captured Michilimackinac and, shortly after, Brock forced the surrender of Detroit. The western part of the continent was in British hands.

Apart from Brock, what other commanders served in the armies protecting Canada?

James Secord was elated by the news of these victories. He had joined his regiment, the lst Lincoln Militia. Fortunately, he was stationed near Queenston, and was able to visit Laura and their children frequently.

"We've got them on the run. They'll never attack us now." But James, too, was wrong.

On October 13, 1812, the people of the Niagara frontier were awakened by the roar of cannon.

British troops had discovered the Americans rowing across the Niagara River under cover of the early morning mist. Under heavy fire from the British guns, some boats were sunk, and emptied their load of soldiers into the fast-running river. However, a number of the Americans managed to cross successfully.

Queenston, for a time, became the centre of the fighting, as American troops moved up from the docks, heading for the heights on the south side of the village.

Laura Secord, with the rest of the village, was soon awakened. With her usual good sense, she had her five children dressed and out of the house in minutes. The eldest was thirteen, the youngest an infant of two. The Secord family went to friends in a nearby farmhouse, away from the shells falling on Queenston. There they waited for news of James Secord and the outcome of the battle.

Brock's ride to Queenston
How does this picture of
General Brock on his horse
Alfred show the urgency of the
situation?

But, unfortunately, the news was all bad. The Americans had firmly secured an excellent position on the heights and were driving the British forces back.

Then the news came that brought despair to everyone. Brock was wounded. Brock was dead. The British army was in full flight.

It took all of Laura Secord's great courage to keep up her own spirits and those of her children. No news came from her husband, whom she knew to be in the thick of the fighting. But bad news about the battle continued to flow in.

Rumours followed rumours. Some said that the Americans had driven the British into panic-filled flight. Others swore the Americans were being driven to their death over the high cliffs lining the Niagara River.

But all agreed that the hero of Upper Canada, General Brock, had been killed. A sharpshooter in the American forces had found Brock an easy target, because of his height and his colourful uniform. As Brock led a handful of men up the steep hill to the United States position, an American soldier stepped from behind a tree, took careful aim and fired.

Almost at the same time came two pieces of information. General Sheaffe had rallied the British troops, the Niagara and York Militias, and a company of Negroes, and routed the Americans.

Word also came that James Secord was badly wounded. He was lying on the battlefield and calling for his wife.

*Sketch map of The Mountain,
Niagara. On top of the
Mountain, the only star fort in
North America was built from
the stones take from the ruins of
Queenston after it was burned
down during the War of 1812*

British uniforms of the War of 1812

General

Captain

Sergeant

Private

C.W.J.

1. How have the American invaders managed to surprise the British?
2. Can you see signs that indicate that the Americans are suffering serious losses?
3. Where do you think Brock fell?
4. How has the artist altered the scene to make his picture more interesting?

The Battle of Queenston, October 13, 1812

Chapter 7 **The Rescue of James Secord**

"Your husband is badly wounded and calling for you, Mrs. Secord." The news was brought by a young soldier, himself barely able to walk.

Such a summons would have made anyone fear the worst. But whenever an emergency arose, Laura Secord met it with courage, energy, and determination. She had helped her father bring a family through the wilderness of New York State. She had helped him, and later her husband, in making their businesses successful. She was not easily discouraged.

So when she heard the report about her husband, she immediately made arrangements for her children to be taken care of and set out for the battlefield.

As she approached the road leading up to Queenston Heights, she saw the dreadful slaughter resulting from the battle. The dead—the red-coated British soldier and the green-uniformed American—lay in strange, twisted positions.

But the dead, at least, were still. It was the wounded, some in a horrible state, that were so terrible to see. The day was coming to an end, and their pitiful cries made even the most hardened wince.

Laura Secord moved slowly up the slope, trying to find her husband. Her heart urged her to help the wounded, but her first duty was to find James.

Suddenly she heard her name, scarcely above a whisper. But, in spite of the noise around her, the sound reached her. She fell to her knees beside her husband. "James, James, are you hurt badly?"

"Badly enough, Laura." He took his blood-stained hand from his shoulder. "A bullet caught me here, Laura. It won't stop bleeding. Can you help me?"

Find out something about army medical services at this time.

There were no medical supplies. Laura ripped a strip of cloth from her petticoat, formed it into a pad, and pressed it against the wound. "Hold it there till we get you home, James. We'll fix it there."

She stood up, looking for someone to help carry her husband home. Without warning, three American soldiers suddenly thrust Laura Secord aside. They were on the point of beating the wounded man to death, when an American officer prevented it and ordered them to carry James Secord to his house.

The Secords long remembered the officer's chivalry during such a bitter struggle. Laura Secord was able to get her husband to the safety of their own house, and care for his wounds there.

Laura Secord's home in Queenston

The day's misfortunes were not over. While Laura was away, the small house at Queenston had been ransacked. What was not stolen, had been smashed. But, again, Laura scarcely gave a thought to this new trouble until she had made her husband as comfortable as conditions allowed.

Before he fell asleep, James turned to his wife. "The General's death is a loss that we shall never recover from. He was a great man. Even as he lay dying, he urged the troops on. 'Push on, York Volunteers,' he said. He would have been proud to see how his men fought."

Laura put her hand on her husband's forehead. "Try to sleep, James. The fighting is over now."

Canada could ill afford the loss of General Brock. However, his courage served as an inspiration to the troops. The British forces suffered reverses, but the eventual victory preserved Canada's right to her own independence.

A grateful country has erected a magnificent monument to the General. It stands on the escarpment, high above the battlefield on which he was killed.

The coat that he wore on that fatal day has been preserved. The bullet hole is easily seen. In the museum at Niagara is General Brock's cocked hat, with its white ostrich plumes, red and white cockade, and gold chain.

Coat worn by Brock when he fell at Queenston. Note the bullet hole

Death robbed Brock of two honours. One was the knowledge that he had been knighted. The other that the hat came too late for him to wear it. He wrote his brother, "All the articles I have ordered have arrived except the cocked hat, for which I am sorry, as on account of the enormous size of my head it is difficult to find a hat to suit me."

Brock was not exaggerating. The inside measurement of the hat is twenty-five inches.

Brock's cocked hat

Chapter 8 **The Long Winter**

McFarland House. This is one of the few houses not destroyed during the War of 1812. What does the house suggest about its owners? What changes can you discover in a modern house, which are not found in this house, almost 200 years old?

A wounded husband, a pillaged and shattered house. It seemed almost too much for one woman to cope with. Everything of value had been taken from the store; almost everything of value had been destroyed or stolen from the house. But Laura Secord never made a habit of pitying herself. There was a job to be done and she did it.

Her first and most important task was to nurse her husband back to health. Not only had he received a musket ball in his shoulder, but his knee had been smashed by another shot. Rest, good food, and care were necessary if he was going to recover.

People in trouble often share what little they have. And so it was during the grim winter of 1812 to 1813. Everyone managed to get enough to eat, but no one had too much. Friendly Indian hunters often brought meat to Queenston. The army spared what it could, and so the little town survived.

People even tried to bring some amusement into their hard lives. When enough men had leave from the army, a dance would be quickly arranged. With someone at the fiddle, and someone calling the steps, for a few hours the war could be forgotten.

Frequently the women met in the afternoons and, knitting or sewing, passed the time in pleasant conversation. Few houses had stoves, so everyone clustered around the fireplace. Women, married or single, wore caps and lace collars, often made of the finest lace obtainable. Weddings were occasions for more dancing and feasting. In this cruel winter of 1812, it was impossible to provide the customary meal, but good fellowship was still there.

Finally, spring came and, with it, the hope that the war would soon end. The pink blossom of the peach trees and the white of the apples were particularly beautiful this spring of 1813, after the miseries of the winter. The people of Queenston planted their fields and gardens, and the memories of the past winter were forgotten.

James Secord was now well enough to sit outside for a few minutes, carefully protected from any cool breeze.

But hopes can be dashed; plans can go astray.

One day in early May, the inhabitants of Queenston again heard the cry, "The Americans have landed."

With unaccustomed speed the Americans soon had control of both sides of the Niagara River. One of their first actions, after occupying the Canadian side, was to round up all men over eighteen and send them as prisoners to the United States. Even such an outstanding figure as the Reverend Robert Addison, the first clergyman on the frontier, was marched away as a prisoner of war, as well as the leading merchants and lawyers of the area. The American General's orders were clear: "Every man of serviceable military age should be considered and treated as a prisoner of war." The order was ruthlessly carried out, and the young, the old, and most of the wounded were sent off. But one glance at the wounded James Secord was enough to show that he could in no way be a threat to the Americans. The wound in his knee had not yet healed and he was unable to walk.

"Let him stay," ordered an officer, conducting the search for men. He looked at the well-cared-for house that Laura Secord took such pride in. "But we'll billet three officers here." He turned to Laura Secord. "We'll need the two rooms upstairs, and prepare dinner for three each day." He pointed to James Secord. "Better get him out of the way. We don't want an enemy soldier listening to us, even though he won't be running to the British with our news."

James Secord did not answer. He was a proud man, and wanted no special treatment, but he was happy that he would not have to leave his wife and young family.

St. Mark's Church, Niagara-on-the-Lake. During the 1812-14 War, the church was used as a hospital and storehouse. This tombstone was used by the army butchers as a chopping block for their meat. It was from this church that the Reverend Robert Addison was taken prisoner. St. Mark's was destroyed with the rest of the village

St. Andrew's Church, Niagara-on-the-Lake, and its box pews

How does this church differ from churches built today? What is the purpose of the box pews? Can you find a picture of a church similar to St Andrew's? Where are most churches of this style built?

A winter dance at home

Skating and skates

C.W. JEFFERYS

Carrioles and sleighs in the early 1800s

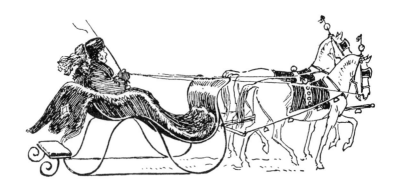

Surprise Attack Chapter 9

The American officers billeted in the Secord house were considerate and helpful. They made certain that a generous supply of food reached the house, so, in this way at least, the family were better off than many of their neighbours.

The Secords were confined to the kitchen and one small bedroom. It was not a large house, and the three American officers had little room in the two small bedrooms upstairs.

The officers soon slipped into the habit of sitting around the dining table after eating and discussing plans and the future of the war. If a housewife and a cripple did chance to overhear them, what damage could be done? No one here was likely to be in touch with the British.

Towards the end of June there was a noticeable increase in the activities and excitement of the American troops.

"They're up to something," said James. "If I could only find out what their plans are."

"Little good would it do you," replied Laura. "You rest and get that leg better. That's the first thing to do."

While they were talking, the door to the kitchen flew open and an American officer entered. For a moment the Secords feared that they had been overheard, but the American had other matters to discuss.

"Mrs. Secord, Colonel Boerstler is taking over command of the American forces at Queenston. We wish to invite him to dinner here tonight. We must have the very best; is that clear?"

Laura Secord burst into loud laughter. "Young man, you forget we are practically your prisoners. Where would we get the best food? We are lucky to get flour for bread, and a piece of beef once a week."

"That's all taken care of. Say what you want and I'll have it delivered. We are depending on you, Mrs. Secord, to do the rest."

True to the officer's word, a variety of food that they had not seen in over a year arrived at the Secords'. There was great activity in the kitchen as everyone, even the younger children, helped their mother.

James' couch was pulled to the wall beside the dining room, to be out of the way. The activities in the kitchen hardly interested him, but he was busy trying to piece together the mumble of conversation of the American officers.

As dusk settled, Colonel Boerstler finally arrived. His loud voice boomed through the small house. "Fine food you young fellows have here. Pretty nice place to spend a war, eh? Well, we'll soon change that. We'll eat first and talk later. But let's not run out of wine. Talking is a dry business."

The dinner was a tremendous success. The Colonel called Laura into the dining room to congratulate her on the meal. "You're spoiling my men, Mrs. Secord, if you feed them like this every day. My compliments, however, on a splendid meal. Now, if you will make sure we will not be disturbed, we shall excuse you, ma'am."

As Laura returned to the kitchen, her husband called her over and whispered, "Keep on with your cleaning up, but don't make too much noise. Something important is going on."

The Secords had not long to wait before the Colonel's voice came through the thin partition as clearly as if he had been in the same room. "We shall move against FitzGibbon at Beaver Dams. That position once captured, the whole of the peninsula is ours. FitzGibbon and Ducharme have raided our outposts and killed our men too long. We have the men and guns to smash FitzGibbon's force, but it must be destroyed before we can move against the British."

The Walk Chapter 10

"We must warn FitzGibbon at Beaver Dams. If he's beaten, or even forced to retreat, nothing will stop the Americans." James Secord looked at his shattered leg. "I can't go. Who can?"

"I'll get to Lieutenant FitzGibbon," said Laura Secord in a voice as soft and ordinary as though she had announced that she was going to the store.

James looked at his wife. Though she had spoken quietly, there was a determination in her voice that would allow no disagreement.

"Laura, it will be a cruel walk, and there'll be danger, but it has to be done. FitzGibbon's 'Green Tigers' have been a constant nuisance to the Americans. His regiment and the Indians are all that is stopping the Yanks from pushing right through the peninsula."

"What shall I tell the Lieutenant when I see him?"

"Tell him that Colonel Boerstler is going to move on Captain DeCew's house with five hundred men and two field guns. They'll move by night, so that gives you a full day to get to FitzGibbon. Surprise is what Boerstler is counting on. If FitzGibbon is warned in time, he'll give the Yanks all the surprise they want."

The longest day in the year had just passed, when Laura started on her journey. She was off shortly after four in the morning, before sunrise.

While neither of the Secords had mentioned the dangers, they were many and they were real. An American sentry might be very suspicious of a woman walking alone toward the enemy lines, and arrest or even shoot her. Rattlesnakes still existed, even though the pigs had routed most of them out from the cultivated fields. Wolves and wildcats were not uncommon. Even more to be feared were unfriendly Indians, who might be found lurking almost anywhere. But perhaps most dangerous of all was the fierce June sun, that could sap the strength of a frail woman on a twenty-mile walk through swamp, brush, and farmland.

Harriet, her seven-year-old daughter, waved good-bye to her mother, who wore a simple dress, a white cotton sunbonnet, and only house slippers to protect her feet. Little did Harriet realize the importance of her mother's journey.

Laura planned to go first to St. David's. This was where James had been raised. In fact, it was named after his eldest brother. Her half-brother, Charles Ingersoll, lived there, at the house of Hannah Secord, the widow of James Secord's brother, Stephen. Though Laura had heard that he was sick, she thought he might be able to finish the walk.

It was not to be. Charles was still too sick even to stand. Hannah dared not leave him. That left only Hannah's daughter, delicate, twenty-year-old Elizabeth, Laura's niece.

"Let me go with you, Aunt Laura," begged Elizabeth. "Two of us need fear no one. I'm sure I can help."

Laura looked at the mother, who nodded her head in assent. So, without any more delay, the two set off.

James had felt that it was wiser to head for Shipman's Corners, rather than try to go directly to Lieutenant Fitz-Gibbon. It was a ten-mile walk through swamp and brush, and, at the best, a dirt road that was little more than a path.

The sun beat down cruelly, and near Shipman's Corners the younger of the two felt she could go no further. The slippers of both women were by now cut to ribbons, and their feet blistered and bleeding. But Laura's only thought was for her niece.

"Just a little further, my dear, and you'll reach a friend's house. You'll be all right there."

Elizabeth realized that she was holding her aunt back. "Thank you, Aunt Laura, I think I must rest."

No time for Laura to bathe her feet in one of the streams across their path; no time to sit in the cool shade to rest. Alone now, Laura turned to the escarpment, another seven miles beyond Shipman's Corners, and continued her steady pace.

Dusk was beginning to fall. She had been walking since four o'clock that morning. Now, almost eighteen hours later, she came to the place called Beaver Dams. Beaver Dams got its name because of the number of beaver that lived in the swampy grounds. Their dams were scattered over a huge area, and the many ponds made walking extremely difficult.

At this time Charles was engaged to be married to Elizabeth Secord, but she died the following year. In 1816, he married Anna Maria Merritt, sister of William Hamilton Merritt, who built the Welland Canal.

There is a legend that Laura Secord pretended to chase her cow, so that she could pass safely through the American lines. Can you suggest reasons why the story of the cow may be either true or false?

At last, Laura managed to pass through the ponds. Her journey was almost over. Now all she had to do was to find DeCew's house, and her mission would be done.

Suddenly, she walked into a group of Indians. Their war cries burst out all around her. "Woman!" they shouted, "Woman!" and shook their tomahawks and pointed their rifles at her. But Laura Secord, frightened though she was, pointed to one of the chiefs.

"Come here. I have important news for Lieutenant FitzGibbon. Take me to him."

To be ordered around by a woman was more than the chief could stand. He turned to walk away, but again Laura repeated her command. There was no doubt of the authority with which she spoke.

The Indians became silent. The chief looked back at Laura. After a moment he said, "Follow me." In a few minutes Laura Secord, tired, drawn, her feet still bleeding, her dress in rags, was ushered into FitzGibbon's headquarters in the DeCew house.

In a few words she gave her message.

John DeCew's house near Beaver Dams, where FitzGibbon and his men had their headquarters

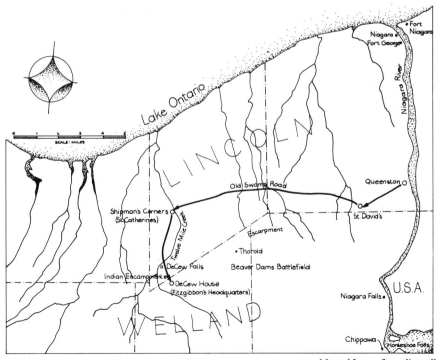

Map of Laura Secord's walk

*Laura Secord tells her story to
FitzGibbon*
*How does this picture suggest
the hardships that Laura Secord
suffered during her walk?*

The Battle of Beaver Dams

Lieutenant FitzGibbon stared at Laura Secord. "Pray sit down, madam. You are far from well, I fear."

"I'm well, sir. It is you who must take care. This very minute large numbers of Americans are approaching, and mean to surprise you and your men."

FitzGibbon nodded. Perhaps he had suspected that such an attack would take place. He spoke quietly, first to one of his aides and then to an Indian. They both nodded and quickly left the room.

"How did you learn this, madam?" asked FitzGibbon, as he turned once more to Laura Secord. "The Americans are many miles from here. How did you obtain the information that you claim to have?"

Laura Secord folded her hands, and in a clear voice recounted the events of the past twenty-four hours. She was so calm that it almost appeared as though she were accustomed to making such trips.

James FitzGibbon

FitzGibbon listened carefully. "Madam, you have done something that few men would dare to do. Pray excuse me. We must see that the Americans get a proper reception." He turned to a newcomer. "Ducharme, how many Indians do you have ready?"

"Forty-one, sir. Twenty-five Caughnawagas and sixteen Mohawks."

Why did the presence of Indians have so much effect on the regular soldiers?

"You will take up your position in the woods at the edge of the escarpment. In the meantime, I will proceed on the road in case they break through your lines." As he prepared to leave, he turned to one of his staff. "Lieutenant Jarvis, see that Mrs. Secord is given anything she wishes."

The room was emptied at once, except for Laura Secord and the Lieutenant.

"If I could have a drink of water and a couch to lie on for a few moments, I would be most grateful."

The Lieutenant got what he was asked for. Laura Secord lay down on a couch and in moments was fast asleep.

She did not know how long she slept. She was awakened by the noise of men shouting and laughing. The room rapidly filled with British soldiers and Indian warriors. A group clustered around FitzGibbon, who was going over every detail of the battle that appeared by now to be over.

As Laura Secord sat up, Lieutenant Jarvis came towards her. "A great victory, madam. A complete victory.

"The Indians caught the Americans in a crossfire and they never did see who was shooting at them. Lieutenant FitzGibbon brought his men up the centre and took the American artillery. Colonel Boerstler was wounded and captured.

"While Boerstler was being asked to surrender, the Lieutenant kept our men marching backwards and forwards, so that the Americans thought we had a huge army. By late afternoon they surrendered—hundreds of them—to a few Indians and a regiment of the line."

A smile lit the face of Laura Secord. The perils and pain of the long walk were all worthwhile.

She was aware that everyone had stopped talking, and all were looking at her. Lieutenant FitzGibbon approached her. He paused in front of her and saluted.

"Mrs. Secord, we have just experienced one of the most complete victories in the history of our army. Madam, the credit for this victory belongs to you."

The battle area

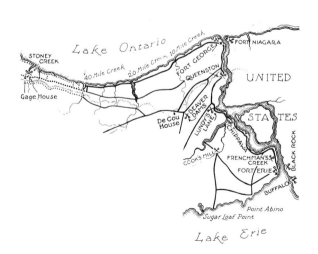

After Chapter 12
the Battle

Even though the number of soldiers that fought at Beaver Dams was not large, the result was of the greatest importance. The victory gave Canada time in which to rearm, and defend her borders. If the Americans had won, they would have captured the whole of the Niagara region. This would have opened up the road to York; the American ships on Lakes Erie and Ontario would have had a great advantage. Indeed, the success or failure of the war could be said to hinge on the results of the Battle of Beaver Dams.

There have been few battles so decisively won. Thirty Americans had been killed and another sixty wounded. In addition, they had lost two cannon, two ammunition wagons, and the weapons of five hundred men. FitzGibbon lost fifteen Indians killed and twenty wounded.

The Indians, quite rightly, were given credit for winning the actual battle. FitzGibbon was praised for his tactics and masterly handling of the troops.

But what of Laura Secord? The fame and fortune that might be expected to reward her brave deed never materialized. Not only was Laura Secord given no recognition, she was, apparently, completely ignored.

But the reasons for this were not hard to discover. Laura's husband, still crippled by his wounds, lay on his sickbed at Queenston. The children, too, were at their home, well behind the enemy lines. It needs little imagination to realize that, if the Americans ever found out about Laura's heroic walk, it would have been a sad day for the Secord family.

Everyone concerned must have agreed to keep quiet about Laura Secord's part in the victory at Beaver Dams. Certainly no one would repeat the story until the Americans were driven out of Queenston.

How Laura on her return journey again avoided the American outposts and returned to her family, we do not know. Perhaps, once again, the appearance of the frail woman in her tattered and dusty dress would make the American sentries believe her to be incapable of doing them any harm.

With little delay Laura returned to her accustomed duties. The most important was to cure her husband. Slowly he was beginning to recover from his dreadful wounds.

But Laura, like the rest of the women of her day, had many other activities.

The garden took a great deal of time and work. The gardener took pride in the bright flowers bordering the walk. But the garden contained more than flowers. Many vegetables, for immediate use and for storing for winter, were grown by the householders. The herb garden provided a surprising variety of herbs that were used not only for cooking, but to cure sickness. The herbs could be dried and saved for the winter. Fruit from the berry bushes and the peach, apple and plum trees was precious, and what was not eaten at once was made into jams and jellies.

Frequently, the women would gather in front of the open fireplace and have either a quilting or a sewing bee. The exchange of gossip, no doubt, helped the time pass quickly. Every house had a big spinning wheel, and spinning was another of the duties of the frontier housewife.

A spinning wheel

Almost every family in the little town owned a cow, and it was the custom for the housewife to milk and care for it.

Fat, grease, and pork rinds were carefully saved in a huge iron kettle. When enough had been collected, a whole day was set aside for soap-making. The lye that was an essential ingredient was made from hardwood ash.

But while the frontier woman worked hard, she also found time to amuse herself. Parties during the long winter nights were frequent. The fiddler called out the reels and dances, and the small houses shook with the gay dancing. Lucky the children who, unseen, could watch the dance from the top of the stairs.

C.W. JEFFERYS

Making soap and potash. What other activities made life for pioneer women so hard?

Spinning, weaving, and quilting bees were occasions for friendly visiting.

Revenge

The capture of Colonel Boerstler and all but six of his soldiers was a bitter experience for a proud army. The loss of almost an entire force had to be avenged. Little wonder that the Secords kept silent about their part in the victory.

Winter came early in that fall of 1813. Snow fell in October and stayed throughout the entire winter. This is most uncommon in the Niagara region. In normal circumstances such a severe winter would have been bad enough, but this particular winter was a tragedy. Niagara-on-the-Lake, Queenston, and Niagara Falls had been pillaged by the American troops. Little of value or comfort had been left. All able-bodied men were either in the army or held prisoner by the Americans.

Food and heat were the two main necessities. Most of the wood cut to last throughout the winter had been stolen. Even the split-rail fences had been used by the soldiers on both sides for fuel.

The American officers no longer used the Secord home at Queenston as a billet. Indeed, all along the frontier they had withdrawn behind their prepared positions.

James Secord, now on the road to recovery, was enthusiastic about this. "You'll see, Laura," he said. "The Yankees will be gone over the river before winter is out. Once they're gone, the war will be as good as over."

But great misfortune and tragedy were still to come before the war ended.

On December 10, 1813, the inhabitants of Niagara were shocked by the shouted announcement of the Americans. "Everyone out. Everyone out. This town will be burned down in fifteen minutes."

Rail splitter and fence viewers

Panic spread as fast as the announcement. What could be saved in fifteen minutes? Furniture was stacked in the snow. The scanty provisions that were to last the winter were piled outside. The sick and wounded were carried out on their beds and left in the snow.

True to their threat, the Americans set fire to every building in the small town. Not even the churches were spared.

As the flames spread, a brilliant glare was reflected in the winter sky. For miles around, people realized the fate of Niagara. And, almost as though by general agreement, their houses were opened to the refugees.

"Thank God, it was not us," said Laura. "We can take in a number of people and be thankful."

After vainly trying to blow up Fort George, the Americans withdrew. Revenge for the senseless burning of Niagara followed within a few days, when Buffalo was put to the flames.

Still the terrible destruction continued. In the summer of 1814, the Americans again started raiding the Niagara area.

Laura was visiting her sister-in-law in St. David's. It was about a year since she had passed through there on her walk to warn FitzGibbon.

The two women sat in the warm July sun, thankful for a little rest from the endless extra duties that the war had brought. Suddenly Laura turned to her sister-in-law. "Hannah, aren't those American soldiers coming towards us?"

Hannah scarcely looked up. "They send a patrol out this way every day. They don't harm anybody and no one bothers them."

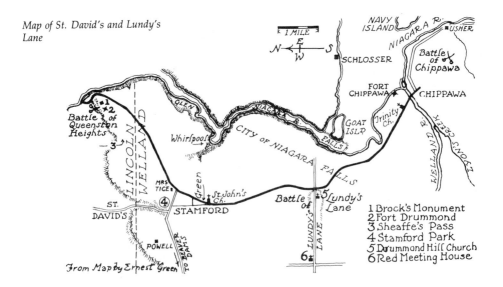

Map of St. David's and Lundy's Lane

1 Brock's Monument
2 Fort Drummond
3 Sheaffe's Pass
4 Stamford Park
5 Drummond Hill Church
6 Red Meeting House

But Hannah had spoken too quickly. The officer in charge of the troop was waving his men on, and shouting at them: "After them. They're British soldiers. Don't let them escape." He pointed to a clump of trees by the road.

A few shots rang out. Nobody was touched, except the officer's horse. An unfortunate shot had caught the poor beast in the head. It was dead before it hit the ground.

The officer was furious. He shook his fist at the Canadian volunteers, who had by now completely disappeared. "You'll pay for this. I'll see to that." He glanced at Laura and Hannah Secord. "You'll pay for this too. The lot of you will be sorry."

Within forty-eight hours, the American colonel's threat was carried out. Once again came the command to leave the houses, and in no time at all St. David's was burning from end to end. This time no one even had the chance to bring their furniture into the streets.

The refugees had to go many miles to find shelter. Some went as far as Hamilton, while others were forced to live in trenches dug in the ground. But Laura was again equal to the demands on her. "We have little, but that we'll share," she said, and she took Hannah and her family into their small home.

The cruel and stupid burning of a town of no military value brought swift punishment to Colonel Stone, the officer responsible, who was dishonourably discharged from the American Army.

The Battle of Lundy's Lane,
July 25, 1814

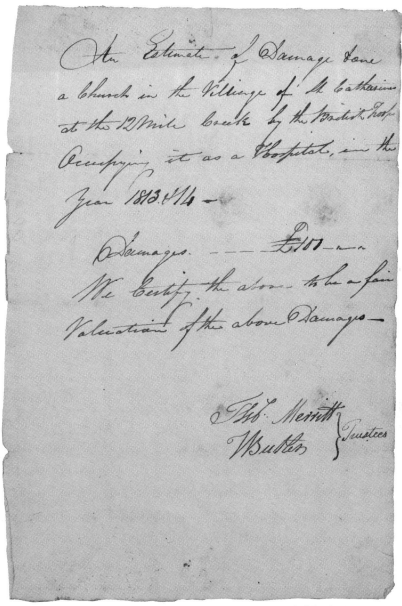

An Estimate of Damage done
a Church in the Village of St. Catharines
at the 12 Mile Creek by the British Troops
Occupying it as a Hospital, in the
Year 1813 & 14 —

Damages. — — — £107 — — —
We Certify the above to be a fair
Valuation of the above Damages —

Tho[s]. Merritt
W Butler   } Trustees

*A claim for damage done to a
village during the war*

Chapter 14 **Forgotten**

Almost twenty years had passed since Laura Secord's courageous walk. The years had not been easy for the Secords, but the family somehow managed to survive, and even to keep growing.

Two daughters, Laura and Hannah, had both been born after the war, and by now were going to be married. Laura, careful and conscientious in everything she did, would not let them leave her house without training in a housewife's skills.

The two girls were busy in the kitchen, making an Indian pudding under Laura's careful eyes.

"Scald the milk, don't burn it, and stir in the meal while it is still boiling. When it's an even thickness, then work in four eggs, a dab of butter, and the berries you picked this morning."

She carefully examined the raspberries that the girls had gathered. "Not very good are they? But they'll have to do. Now stir gently, Laura, or there'll be lumps all through the pudding. And, most important: dip the pudding in a pan of cold water as soon as it is out of the oven, and then your pudding will never stick to the cloth. That's all for now, girls. Wash up, and we'll have the pudding for dinner tonight."

She turned to her husband, James, who had been watching the lesson from the door. "What do you want, James? Is your Court not in session?"

"Aye, it is, and I'll be getting back at once, but I wanted to show you this petition that brother David is sending to the government. You don't have to read it all; just this part here."

Laura read the section James pointed out:

In 1828, James Secord had been appointed Registrar of the Niagara District Surrogate Court. In 1833, he was promoted to Judge.

"I am now an old man broken down with trouble and disappointment and reduced by the war. Much better would it have been for all those unhappy sufferers by the late war, had they never been promised payment, than promised and not paid.

"I was in every battle of magnitude fought on the lines within the District of Niagara during the late war, namely—the Battle of Queenston, Chippawa, Lundy's Lane, Fort Erie, and the capture of Colonel Boerstler at Beaver Dams.

"However our faith is still strong in the Government to whom we owe our allegiance and trust that it will reward the efforts we made during the late war."

Laura handed back the letter. "Little good will ever come of it, I'm sure. What has the government done for us? You still suffer from your wounds. Our home was pillaged twice, and we have never been able to refurnish it, even with the cheapest things. I say let's forget the government, for certainly they have forgotten us."

James smiled. "I've another bit of news. If you've stopped scolding the government, I'll give it to you. I've just been offered the post of Collector of Customs at Chippawa. It means giving up the Surrogate Court, but it also means almost two hundred pounds a year. What do you think, Laura?"

Laura sat down. "What do I think? Why, take it, James. Take it before you lose the chance."

"It means that I won't have the position that I have now as Judge in Court."

"You can't eat position, and you can't buy dress material with it."

"And we'll have to move to Chippawa, but there's a fine house there that goes with the job."

Tears came into Laura's eyes. After so many years of struggling to raise a large family on a tiny income, the future now promised at least comfort.

She quickly brushed her tears away and smiled at her husband. "We'll leave tomorrow, if they're ready for us in Chippawa."

Chapter 15 **Mackenzie's Rebellion**

William Lyon Mackenzie

In 1837, rebellion broke out in Upper Canada. William Lyon Mackenzie raised a body of men who felt they could no longer get justice from the government or the law. Although Chippawa was far from the skirmish in Toronto, news came that the rebellion had been crushed and Mackenzie was a hunted fugitive.

James was happy to announce the defeat of the rebels. "It was your old friend, Colonel FitzGibbon, who scattered the rascals. An idle group they are, too. I hope they're all punished."

Laura recalled her meeting with the Colonel. "He was a fine man, James. Perhaps one of these days we'll meet him again."

As the family sat down to dinner, there was a furious knocking on the door. "Open the door," shouted a loud voice. "Open up, or we'll blow the door down."

James rushed to the door, and flung it open. A corporal stood there, with four soldiers, their guns cocked. "Must search your house at once. Warrant here."

James stood aside, and the soldiers entered. Their search was soon over. As they were leaving, James asked, "What's the trouble, Corporal? Whom are you looking for?"

"Mackenzie, the rebel, was reported coming through here. If we don't catch him now, he'll slip over the border into the United States. Slippery fellow, he is."

But Mackenzie escaped. He and a small group of his followers managed to reach Navy Island in the Niagara River, just upstream from Chippawa.

The rebels' two-starred flag could be seen waving over the camp that was provided with both men and supplies from the American side of the river. The ship *Caroline* was the rebels' link with the Americans. Carefully avoiding Canadian waters, she continued to ship supplies day after day.

Trade came to a halt in Chippawa, and so did James Secord's income.

"If the *Caroline* can be sunk, the rebels are finished. Otherwise, in another month Mackenzie will have a force to be reckoned with," said James Secord to his wife. "We'll help if we can, and I think we can. I've been asked to keep a fire burning at the mouth of the Chippawa River. But not a word, Laura, to anyone."

There was a great deal of coming and going. Although the Secords never heard any details, they were sure that the fire burning on the beach had something to do with the *Caroline*.

One cloudy night a boat, commanded by Captain Drew, slipped from the Canadian shore. Before the rebels were aware of its presence, the crew had cut the cables of the *Caroline* and set her on fire. The strong current of the Niagara River quickly carried her to the falls, where she was swept to her destruction.

The burning Caroline, going over the falls, December 29, 1837

Angry notes from the Americans about this attack on one of their ships in their own waters were sent to the Canadian government. But nothing came of their complaints, and Mackenzie was forced to quit Navy Island.

For a year there were incidents, as the rebels continued to make raids across the border. James Secord, as Her Majesty's Customs Collector, was in an exposed position. However, slowly the sparks of rebellion were quenched, and no harm came either to James Secord or his family.

Navy Island

Rebels, 1837.
This picture of rebels moving on
Toronto suggests many reasons
why their rebellion was doomed
to failure. How many can you
find?

Chapter 16 The Passing Years

Although getting on in years, Laura never lost her courage when she felt duty beckoned her.

One summer day, James came home with the news that a party of smugglers was to make a landing on the Canadian shore that very evening.

"James, you cannot arrest them. They'll be desperate men. What can you do alone?"

"I'll be all right, Laura," he replied. "John, my deputy, will be there. It would be nice to have a third, but at this late hour it can't be done. We'll manage, I'm sure."

Laura thought for a moment. She was plainly unhappy at the idea of her husband facing such a dangerous situation. Suddenly she turned. "You'll have your third man, James. Don't be afraid that you won't get a volunteer."

"Now Laura, there's no one I can get. I've told you that. Where's this third man to come from?"

"I'll do it, James," and she laughed at the look on her husband's face. "I'll dress as a man, and carry a gun, too. But don't load it, it might go off in my hands."

And Laura Secord did just that. In a long overcoat, with a cap pulled over her ears, and carrying a wicked-looking gun, she stood by her husband as he arrested two very surprised smugglers.

Laura's granddaughter, who remembered this story, also had high praise for her grandmother as a nurse. Once, for three months she never went to bed, but sat beside her husband's bed in an armchair.

Over the years her family grew up, married, and moved away. But it seemed that there was always a responsibility for Laura to shoulder. Two of her daughters were widowed; so each, with a young family, moved back into the Secord home at Chippawa.

With a small pension from the army and his earnings as Collector of Customs, James managed to provide for his family. Laura took pride in the dresses she made for her daughters and grandchildren, and in her cooking, which was still famous.

More than once Laura Secord presented a petition to the government, asking for either money or a government post, in return for her services to her country. For a time she had high hopes of being put in charge of the newly built monument to Brock. Indeed, she had been promised the post, but the tragic death of a judge, Colonel Nichol, leaving a widow and four children, meant that once again she was disappointed. The position was given to Mrs. Nichol, who needed it even more.

Presenting a petition was a far more common custom in those days and regarded as a quite proper way to make a request.

One of James petitions starts:

James Secord humbly sheweth

That your petitioner is one of the oldest inhabitants of this province, has numerous relatives in the British Army, is Brother-in-Law to the Honorable Richard Cartwright, is Captain in the second Regiment of Lincoln Militia, was wounded at the battle of Queenston, and twice plundered of all his moveable property. That his wife embraced an opportunity of rendering some service at the risk of her life, in going thro' the Enemies Lines to communicate information to a detachment of His Majesty's Troops at the Beaver Dams . . . .

This petition was unsuccessful, so the Secords got FitzGibbon to add a note to another petition. This is what he wrote:

I certify that Mrs. Secord did in the month of June, 1813, come to the Beaver Dam and communicate to me information of an intended attack to be made by the Enemy upon the Detachment then under my command. This information was substantially correct. Mrs. Secord arrived at my Station about sunset of an excessively warm day, after having walked about twelve miles which I at the time thought was an exertion which a person of her slender frame and delicate appearance was unequal to make.

James FitzGibbon
Captn. Half Pay

Seventeen years later FitzGibbon wrote another petition. This time it had some effect. The sum of one thousand pounds was given—not to Laura Secord but to FitzGibbon.

Many years later the *Niagara Mail*, a local newspaper, had this to say about Laura Secord:

"She had done her country more signal service than half the soldiers and militiamen engaged in the war. We say the brave, loyal old lady not only be allowed to sign the address but she deserves a special introduction to the Prince as a worthy example of the fire of 1812 when both men and women vied alike in the resolution to defend their country."

Brock's monument at Queenston Heights. This is the third monument on this site. The first, begun in 1824, was torn down when it was found that a copy of William Lyon Mackenzie's newspaper, the Colonial Advocate, was in the foundation stone. The second was blown up by Irish rebels in 1840. The third, completed in 1856, is shown here. If you climb to the top, you have a magnificent view of the Niagara River.

It has been said of the Battle of Beaver Dams that "The Mohawks did the fighting, the Caughnawagas got the plunder and FitzGibbon got the praise."

And Laura Secord got nothing.

However, the family managed to live well. It was a closely knit group and a very happy one.

But tragedy struck, far greater than the loss of money. James Secord died in 1841, aged sixty-eight. Laura was left a widow at sixty-five.

Fame Comes to Chapter 17
Laura Secord

With the death of James, the income from Customs and the small pension were both cut off. Laura was penniless. But, strengthened by courage and an unquenchable faith, she was never discouraged too long.

It is likely that her fine needlework brought in some money, and her large family would contribute more. For a time she ran a school for children. She had a little property, and so, once again, Laura Secord managed to survive.

Slowly, recognition of her brave act grew. A newspaper article gave her full credit for FitzGibbon's victory. FitzGibbon wrote another statement of her actions so many years before. And Laura Secord's own account now became more detailed. She wrote:

"I found great difficulty in getting through the American guards, which were ten miles out in the country. Determined to persevere I left early in the morning, walked nineteen miles over a rough and difficult part of the country where I came to a field belonging to Mr. DeCew. Here I found all the Indians encamped; by moonlight the scene was terrifying. They all rose and yelled 'Woman' which made me tremble."

Finally, when she was eighty-five years old, Laura Secord received part of the recognition she deserved.

In 1860, the Prince of Wales, eldest son of Queen Victoria and heir to the throne, was visiting Canada. Like any other visitor to the Niagara Peninsula, he was shown Niagara Falls. Laura and her daughter, Charlotte, stood patiently waiting his arrival and cheered and waved as he passed them.

Prince Albert Edward never forgot his first view of the falls. Nor did he ever forget the show put on by Blondin, the tightrope walker, crossing and recrossing the rapids on a tightrope. First, the daring Frenchman carried a man on his back; then he returned walking on stilts.

Before returning home, the Prince unveiled a large stone that marked the spot where Sir Isaac Brock had fallen at the Battle of Queenston Heights.

Laura had hoped to be presented to the Prince, but was disappointed. Once again, she presented a petition, pointing out her age, her service, and that of her late husband. Once again, Colonel FitzGibbon attached a kind note to the petition.

Brock's monument. James Secord was rescued by Laura near this stone that marks the spot where Brock fell, killed by an American sniper. The hill to the top is quite steep. Was Brock's charge up the hill the action of a brave man or an act of great rashness?

When the Prince returned to England he sent gifts to many of those who had petitioned him. One of these was for Laura Secord: one hundred pounds in gold. After nearly fifty years, recognition at last came to this great Canadian heroine.

One more battle was to take place near Laura. This was the brief invasion of the peninsula by a mob of Irish rebels, who wanted to strike at Britain through Canada. We may be sure that Laura regarded this invasion with courage and the conviction that her country would soon triumph.

Fame had come too late to change Laura Secord's life in any way. She still did her housework; well over ninety years old, tiny and frail-looking, she could do more than many people years younger than she.

With her children and grandchildren, Laura Secord's last years were spent in a quiet and calmness that she had not always known.

Laura Secord died in 1868, at the age of ninety-three.

A plaque on the school in Queenston that bears her name has this inscription:

Laura Secord monument, Queenston Heights

LAURA SECORD MEMORIAL

IN LOVING AND HONOURED MEMORY OF

LAURA INGERSOLL SECORD

A RESIDENT OF QUEENSTON AND

A HEROINE OF UPPER CANADA

WHO SAVED HER COUNTRY

FROM THE ENEMY IN 1813.

A Gentlewoman in Upper Canada: the Journals of Anne Langton. Toronto: Clarke, Irwin, 1950.

History of Niagara, Janet Carnochan. Toronto: William Briggs, 1914.

Isaac Brock, Hugh Eayrs. Toronto: Macmillan Co. of Canada, 1924.

Laura Secord, The Legend and the Lady, Ruth McKenzie. Toronto: McClelland & Stewart, 1971.

The Story of Laura Secord and Canadian Reminiscences, Emma A. Currie. St. Catharines, Ontario, 1913.

A Veteran of 1812: The Life of James FitzGibbon, Mary Agnes FitzGibbon (granddaughter). Toronto: Coles Publishing Company, 1970. (First published in 1894.)

Winter Studies and Summer Rambles in Canada, Anna Jameson. Toronto: McClelland & Stewart, 1965 (paperback). (First published in 1838.)

Credits   The authors wish to acknowledge the assistance and encouragement of a number of friends which have made this brief biography, and others in the series, possible. Special thanks must be given to Mrs. S. Wilson of the St. Catharines Public Library; Mrs. C. Roy of the Lincoln County Board of Education; Mr. A. Ormston, Curator of the St. Catharines Museum.

The publishers wish to express their gratitude to the following who have given permission to use copyrighted illustration in this book:

The Buffalo and Erie County Historical Society, page 46.
Collins + World Publishing, pages, 40, 48.
Mr. Charles P. de Volpi, Page 52.
The Metropolitan Toronto Central Library, pages 12, 22-23, 25, 35, 37.
The Public Archives of Canada, pages 2, 4-5, 6, 7, 8, 10, 11, 18, 20, 21, 25, 28, 29, 30, 36, 38, 41, 43, 44, 50.
St. George's Church, St. Catharines, page 47.

Editing: Laura Damania
Design: Jack Steiner
Illustration: Frank Loconte

Mr. John M. Bassett is Consultant — Communications, and Mr. A. Roy Petrie is Superintendent — Operations, at the Lincoln County Board of Education.